Players in the Dream:
Dreamers in the Play

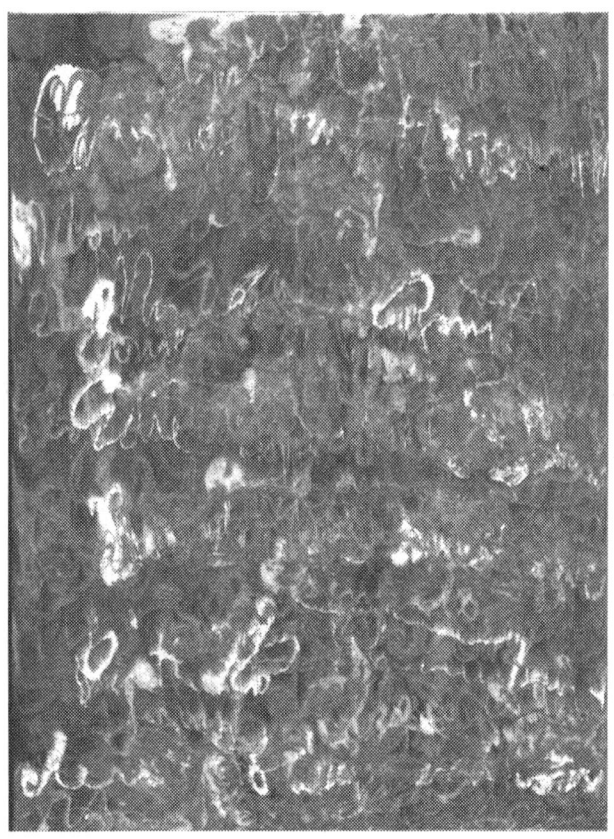

Marian Kaplun Shapiro

Plain View Press
P. O. 42255
Austin, TX 78704

plainviewpress.net
sbright1@austin.rr.com
512-440-7139

Copyright Marian Kaplun Shapiro, 2006. All rights reserved.
ISBN: 978-1-891386-72-5
Library of Congress Number: 2006938132

Cover "Remembrance" © Rebecca Susan Woodhouse, 2006.

Author photo by Stuart Dickstein.

Acknowledgements

Advice, Inspiration, *Animus*; Deconstruction, *Cezanne's Carrot*; Last Assignment, *Cuivre River Anthology*; Assessment Instrument, Just Desserts, *Eye*; Cycle, *Fresh*; Ouija Board, *Ibbetson Press*; Mayday, *Homestead Review*; Assessment Instrument, *Incliner*; Monkey Mind, *Inquiring Mind*; Never Again, Vedran Smailovich, *Language And Culture*; Memorial Service For A Quaker, Naming, *Lotus Blooms*; Inheritance, REM, *Manorborn*; The Sculpture Garden, *Margie*; Stonehenge, Letter To King Tut, Keepsake, Birthday, Leaves; *Miranda*; Bed, *Oasis*; Annual Pigeon Shoot, *Out Of Line*; From Afar (In Maine), *Open Windows Anthology*; Elegy, *Pebble Lake Review*; In The Season Of Miracles,*Pedestal*; Reincarnation, *Penwomanship*; The Reason, *Potpourri*; April In Paris: Sur Le Metro, Choosing A Seat, Before I Landed, *Prism Quarterly*; Kaddish For September, Synesthesia, *Promise*; Strange Meeting II, *Reed*; Where The Wild Things Are, *Revolve*; September 11, 2001, *Reynard anthology*; ER, IV, EKG, CAT, BP...*Re)Verb*; Impact, *Rockhurst Review*; Moose Run, New York City, *Sacred Bearings*; Packing, *Slate And Style*; View From A Train Window, *Smartish Pace*; Inside Looking Out, *Somerville News*; Elevators, *Sow's Ear*; From Afar (In Maine), *This Hard Wind*; Kaddish For September, September 11, 2001, *Types And Shadows*; Elevators, *Weavers Of Dreams anthology*; Flat Earth (earlier version), *Why Can't You See Me? (Inglis House)*; Pure Love, *Wild Goose*; Little Ghost, *Manorbom*.

Contents

Part 1: *Hyphen*   7

Introduction	9
Monkey Mind	10
Before I Landed	11
Fragment	12
REM	13
Starting From Here	14
Synesthesia	15
Theme and Variation	16
Basic Arithmetic	17
Impact	18
Watching Grass Grow	19
Reincarnation	20
Flat Earth	21
Threats & Promises, Promises & Threats	22
Ouija Board	23
The Reason	24
Anemnesis	25

Part 2: *Holding Truth Still*   27

"Where Were You When I Laid . . .	29
View From A Train Window	30
Where The Wild Things Are	31
Elevators	33
In the Season of Miracles	34
Guide	35
Just Desserts	37
Never Again, Vedran Smailovich	38
Studying a Film on the Treatment of Burns	40
Annual Pigeon Shoot, Higgens, PA.	41
Inside Looking Out	43
Nightmare	44
Letter to King Tut	45
Strange Meeting II	47
September 11, 2001	48
Kaddish for September	49
"If you can't say something nice, . . .	51
Mayday	52

Moose Run River, New York City	53
Psalm 10B	55
Progress	56
Elegy	57
Memorial Service for a Quaker	58

Part 3: *and*   61

Mobile	63
Cycle: Alfred, Maine	64
Quaker Meeting: Cambridge/Rangeley, Maine	65
Assessment Instrument	67
From Afar (In Maine)	68
Naming	70
Deconstruction: 'I Know Why The Caged Bird Sings"	72
Calling	75
Bed	76
Advice	77
Little Ghost	78
ER, IV, EKG, CAT, BP...	79
Time Travel	80
Birthday	82
Visitation	83
April in Paris: Sur Le Metro	84
La Touriste San Souci	86
Ice Season on the Reservoir	87
Last Assignment (*with guitar*)	88
Keepsake	89
Packing	90
Choosing a Seat	91
Pure Love	92
After	93
Inheritance	94
The Sculpture Garden	95
Enjambment	97
Leaves	98
Ellipses	99
Life	100
About the Author	101

Dedication

To my husband Irwin

My ever-helpful helpmate, constant supporter, cheerleader, fan-club, and loving companion for the incredibly short time of 47 years...and still counting.

Part 1

Hyphen

Introduction

I
kite
earth-sky
string pulled taut, exquisite
hyphen between mute boundaries.

Monkey Mind

rising
      falling
           rising   wedding
                falling
     later   *rising*   e-mail
                   falling
                      rising
    what if   *falling*   rain
                  rising
              falling
          rising
       falling
    rising   lunch
falling
   rising
     falling
       rising
  yesterday   *falling*
           rising
             falling
           rising
        falling
  once   *rising*
     falling
   rising
  falling
rising
   falling
     rising   maybe
       falling
        rising
          falling
        rising
       falling
      rising
    falling
   rising
  falling

Before I Landed

"for the silence and words have been of one texture, one piece."
Thomas R. Kelly, The Gathered Meeting, 1940

Before I landed

music and silence were inseparable

space and I were married by the clouds

the spoken word was danced   and

dancing   was painted in the colors

of *never-seen* and *never-been*.

Sometimes

I catch an inkling of that daynight from the lemonade ghost-moon in the timeless sky. Cool cool light, come to my open window. Remind me of the *once* upon a time before life taught us about the end of it.

Fragment

Rains I dream of always fall —
Why is it when I dream of stars,
the sea becomes sky,
the sky the ocean?

REM

    images drop like   acid

        rain   rain

            into

theplainsofsleep   theplainsofsleep

with and without words   poems of past

pain   pop   like birthday balloons

meeting up with dragon   flies

    Come back!

    Dawn breaks a
    handpainted slender-
    necked cruet full
    of garden parties, wedding
    toasts and baby-
    showers shattering
    into shards of sun-
    sets. Lover,

    tell me *your* dream
    tell me *your* poem

Starting From Here

(reading in Rangeley, Maine)

Your way-cool far-out poems blast me beyond
       the dock onto
        the rotors of
      a robo-helicopter from
      another galaxy, whizzing off
    to rendezvous with

    a shape-
             shifting
                        silvery
                                    hot
                                                      air
                                      balloon
                           shimmying
                           up

Oquossoc way
    (up the hill, I mean,
    one mile North of here
    on Rte. 4).

Drop me off at Koob's
Garage. Re-alignment
is their specialty. They
might as well touch up
a few dents and check
the oil while they're at it,
a good idea before beginning
any long trip.

Synesthesia

spirals of dream   and
photograph of symphony
painting of sonnet   sand
poem of singing star
dancing out-breath   frozen
fossil flame   moon-
branch   etched
stave of Arctic stone   in
Agra, in Angkor Wat,
in Isfahan, in
your timeless   hand.

Theme and Variation

You don't know that
> I'm turning cartwheels in your dining room
> napping in your bathtub
> whistling on your roof, playing
> hide-and-seek in your bookcase
> between the pages
> between the sheets
> under the rug.

You don't know that
> I know that
> this is a game for blind deaf mutes.
> The rules are unspoken.
> The pieces are invisible.
> The dreamers are players in the dream.
> The players are dreamers in the play.

Basic Arithmetic

One and
    one make two
        ones. You
            know what I

mean: The story/
    poem is a dream/
        the dreams I told
            you/you

told me. One
    and one make
        two ones and
            two twos. You

know what I mean.

            for Sandy's festshrift
            12/30/90

Impact

    The case remains open
    after a billion years.
    The evidence piles up, is

sifted   weighed

    accepted   disregarded

  arguments   for

          and   against

passionate   proposals

    flying

through   the

centuries, asteroids and comets
of certainty burning up
on schedule.

        The case
remains open: The *what ifs*
sing their siren songs.
What happened? When?

    and   why   ?

Watching Grass Grow

it must happen when we blink or
in that mid-yawn moment when
sound is whited out by inbreath,
when we doze in the afternoon,
or while shopping at the Super
Stop & Shop. Perhaps it's growing
madly in the night. Perhaps
it sprouts lickety split between
the eggroll and the scallion chicken
at the Chinese restaurant,
or when we're looking the other way,
in no time flat, exclaiming at
the sudden redness of a baby cardinal
on the greening oak-branch, or
shouting at the squirrel greedily
scarfing down the oiled sunflower seed
at the birdfeeder.

We know how grass makes fools
of us, we who have been children.

Reincarnation
(a conversation)

Where is your cat, Grammy?
She died.
Why?
She was very old and sick. In the spring,
when the ground is soft, we can bury her.

And then will she grow up again?

Flat Earth

The earth is flat. I know.
I have seen its edge
with my own eyes. My toes
have curled around its rim
like an eagle's talons. In
the next life I will ask for wings
like hers.

Threats & Promises, Promises & Threats

I will love you forever.
I will never lie to you.

I will never lie to you.
I will love you forever.

Ouija Board

We would like to know what you have in store for us.
What will we get for Christmas?
Who will we marry when we grow up?
If we are very very good, will we get our hearts' desire?

Sit down with me, across the ouija board,
resting your fingers lightly on the pointer. Be
patient. Soon it moves, moves, all by itself.

Some say your wishes are like tides, pulled
by invisible forces against your helpless fingers.
But we believe in magic, because we see
the answers spelled out before our hungry eyes.

The Reason

Grandfather is dead.
He died because
he did not finish his orange
juice. I know because the glass
is there, half-full
beside the bed.

Anemnesis

             "What
         does your father do?"
      It's 1944. Kindergarten.
    I am 5. "He types," I answer. (So
     much for mothers.) (So much for academia.)
    "And what do you want to be when you grow up?"
   "A painting man!" O to ride on scaffolds high in the Bronx
 air, to transform housing project window sills from grey to green, to
yellow, or darkest purple-red with my very own painting brush. O to be
6! 7! To read! and write! and ride a bike! I am a girl who can do anything!

                8,9,10,11. Things have changed.
                Nightmares happen. Newsreels document
                skeletons stacked like naked Xmas trees
                raped of their tinsel and their ornaments,
                corpses on the frozen curbside, waiting
                for the garbage truck. Children have been
                burned in ovens like french fries. 12,
                13, 14, 15. Lynchings. Holocausts
                of every shape and size. With personal certainty
                I know how it could happen, how it happened
                and will happen and will happen, world
                without end. 16, 17, 18, 19.
                Still, I count by 1's. Unraveling
                takes a long time. I can do anything
                but that.

20. We count by decades now.
Ready or not, I marry. Love invites me
to the ball. Surprised, I learn to waltz,
a little awkwardly. Two children are born
a boy; a girl. They are beautiful. 30.
40. They grow up. Middle age
takes out a mortgage on my hair, my skin. I
remember everything. 50. Still,
everything matters. A grand-daughter giggles
underground arpeggios tickling
my heart of hearts. Fountains of birdsong bubble
rainbows at my window feeder. So
I come to see that Project pigeons are
the tough, tenacious cousins of my beloved
mourning doves.

60. 61. The year 2000 has arrived and gone, with all its 0's opening their
hungry mouths of possibility. Counting by ones again. Peace comes
to visit. Space makes friends with me. I read. I type my poems.
I am touched by the impossible. I learn to rest. I shop
for paint pots: green, yellow, and darkest purple-
red. I will transform the waiting window
sills with my very own brush. In this
new century I am again
a girl who can do
anything.

Part 2

Holding Truth Still

"Where Were You When I Laid the Foundations of the Earth?"

*God, in **Job** 38:4*

    I am uncolor
    unshape
    unmind

    I am not
    who
    what

Even air is hard as a floor in the house of living.

    before sunrise
    is sun
    unlight?

    I am unspace
    no
    where.

View From A Train Window
(or, View From A Dream)

Passing over the wild Mystic River
in Connecticut I note the seven
story box factories with their broken
windows competing for air space
with wondrous pterodactyls soaring over-
head. The great wooly mammoths sitting
on their haunches watch six spangled
bison leap in mating dances while
naked men, beautiful as Botticelli
angels cavort among the waves which roll
and butt against the beach. You are
among the swimmers. You are also sitting
next to me, sedately reading your paper-
back. There is nothing strange about
your being in two places at once, or
about the red hair you, in the water,
have sprouted. I wonder about the meaning
of sleep. Who sleeps? Who has woken?

Where The Wild Things Are

      Three men are storming the house
      One man is lurking in the street
      The wolf is knocking at the door
(His snout is worming through the safety chain)
      The sirens are baying. The bombs are falling.
      I am telling the truth
(I am not telling the truth. The truth can kill you)
      The police are not coming
      No one is coming
      The elevator stops between floors
(Write 100 times: never go with strangers)
      (Taxi drivers don't count. Teachers don't count)
      The doctor plants his penis in a bowl
(I'm making that up) I CAN'T BREATHE!
      Mommy has turned into a wolf. I
      am going to be eaten all up.
      The wolf is in the stairwell
(Write 100 times: I will not play in the stairwell)
      Secret passages lace basement to basement
      (if one door locks there is no way out)
      (no one will ever find you)
(Write 100 times: I will not play in the basement)
      The sirens mean take cover under the desks
      The fire alarms mean leave your belongings and
      march out quietly, quietly. The wolf
      is under the bed, waiting.
(Write 100 times: walk, do not run. No talking!) (SHUT UP!)
      (Don't say shut up.) (Don't tell.)
      The hanged man dangles from the bedroom
      shade. The turkey sleeps in the ventilator.
      The taxi driver strokes a shrunken head,
      a human prune, a trophy on a keyring.
      I vomit by the side of the road.
      People whisper, people cry

(Children are being burned alive in Auschwitz, in Hiroshima.
　　　Don't worry. That's far away.)
　　　I'm on the wrong subway/bus/train.
　　　Quicksand will swallow me up. Slowly,
　　　slowly, it sucks me into the ooze.
　　　It is licking at my chin. Wake up!
(Write 100 times:Keep your mouth shut. Keep your mouth shut)
　　　Skulls are pyramided by the side of the road
　　　(Small, medium, and large) Line up in size places.
　　　The wolf is opening the latch; soon
　　　he will, at last, get in.
　　　The telephone is broken.
　　　The telephone is dead. I am falling, falling. (My,
what big teeth you have, grandma!) (The better to eat you with)
　　　People are exploding like firecrackers.
　　　People slip away. No one says goodbye.

　　　I'm lost again. Stairs exit onto hospital
　　　wards, and my car has disappeared.
　　　The elevator rockets towards the roof
(Do not use the elevator alone till you can reach the alarm)
　　　I seem to have killed somebody. (Don't worry)
　　　The sky is falling. You are ten feet tall.
(Write 100 times: Cheer up. Tell the truth.Smile and say thank you)
　　　My pocketbook has been stolen/lost.
　　　My teacher sits me on his lap. I forget his name.
　　　(Teachers don't count. Doctors don't count)
　　　Wandering in the spiral of the parking garage
　　　the wolf lurks behind the stanchions.
　　　I am a rabid dog, foaming and growling.
　　　Watch out for Charles -
　　　He sets fire to girls' long hair.
　　　No one knows why.

Elevators

sometimes the doors close
me out, and he dissolves
into the updown black box,
or they close me in before
he gets on, or they open be-
tween floors, or they do
not open at all...some nights
the elevator blasts off right
through the roof, or hurtles
to the basement....and
pressing the emergency button
never does any good.

In the Season of Miracles

Surprise! A dolphin turns into
a wolf. A killer sheep
keeps watch on the horizon, lest
we forget, lest we forget. Where
is the gunman/warrior? The aborigine
is now an opthalmologist
who drives a truck/bus/moving van/
taxi/subway train. Now he
becomes a roadrunner, laughing
stock of the cuckoo

family. Where is the laundry man? Who
speaks Yiddish in Beirut? Why
did you fire bomb the cable car?
The bulldog roller-skates as lilacs
perfume the December snow.
The chorus screams; the smoke alarm
sings lullabyes. Above
the piazza a sharp-beaked bird
of paradise dangles two chickens
from its webby feet.

My head is hurted.
Take me with you.

Guide

Dropping pebbles we
make our way. Only at deepest night
can such a fearful holy pilgrimage
be undertaken. You hold the flashlight,
I hold the map. You have learned
the language of bushes, leaves, and trees,
compasses and jacknives.
You, old boyscout, confidently scan
the sky, point and declare:
The stars will lead us there!

You don't know much.
You don't know about the holes that reach
all the way to China, and the viper
coiling in the robin's nest. One
step to the right a landmine lies
in wait for you. And there
are many more, should you
somehow miss the ditch of quicksand, or
the werewolf sucking blood
beneath the forest floor.

Behold the witch! Behold
her poisoned chocolate cookie house! We
call a trial: I sentence her to death.
You nod agreeably. Shall we burn
her to ashes, as the story tells
us to? Chop her to pieces? Throw
her to the lions? Bash
her head against the rocks? Patiently,
you wait, light in hand.
It's all the same to you.

continued

It's not the same to me.
Exhausted, I sleep, dreamless in the grass.
You stand watch, my valiant brother, my
fourteen stalwart angels. Come the morning
we set out, hand in hand
for home, counting pebbles,
singing in the sun.
The witch has vanished, like the Pleiades,
into the dawn air.
I am hungry, and

I eat the lethal cookies
one
by
one.

Just Desserts

There are hands I'd like to amputate
   fingers I would crush with my boots, eyes
I would put out, necks, and arms, and legs
   and breasts and penises I would smash
with hammers, shovels, and baseball bats.
My gossamer dress will be spattered like a surgeon's smock.
Blood, and shreds of flesh and bone are in my job
      description, along with kisses, wedding rings,
      and golden eggs.

I am the Good Fairy.
I arrange for Cinderella to marry the prince,
   and on the very nuptual day, send birds
   to blind her selfish stepsisters. HURRAH!
When Rumpelstiltskin has his final tantrum I split
   his swollen body right down the middle.
        SO MUCH FOR HIM!
When the giant, that cannibal, makes his fool-
   hardy way down the beanstalk, Jack
      is waiting with my ax. SMASH!
And what a triumph for Gretel! She shoves
      the cunning witch into her own oven, and
         all the world cheers her desperate screams.
But their wicked mother, who sent her children
      into the forest to starve as they wandered
        lost and terrified -
I did not dare design her properly horrible fate. No.
I said, merely, "She died." That's all.
Ah, more would be too much for the children
who have already suffered more than we can know.

Never Again, Vedran Smailovich

Twenty-two years ago
  at this very desk, the sun
      gliding gently through the window
         warming me with May, I
            became one of *them*: Deliberately,
               I murdered 47 wasps, one
at a time, as each slow-danced
  across the landscape of my paper
      work. With practice I got better
         at it, my new career:
            cloth instead of kleenex. A certain
               grip, a certain satisfaction counting

corpses. I know, Vedran. Once upon a time we children stood before
our mirror, arms and neck aching, desperate suitors of our reluctant
  violin/cello bow. Double stops. Arpeggios. After
    years and centuries we coax the overtones of Bach's
      astounding love into the bombed out air. Peace!
        Peace! Stop here and listen! This is
       the Second Coming. This is the Law
      of Laws. Music stands
        us up like
        a tree.

Today it's carpenter ants. Bounding
  from the baseboard, instant black
      refugees, they dodge the smart-bomb
         of my size 8 shoe. They
             recognize my old rap-sheet, my murderer's
                M.O., a serial killer saying kaddish,

calling me with those most holy
  words: *Peace. Truth.* Tonight
     I find myself waking
        to another nightmare that
            was not a dream. NO! NEVER AGAIN!
                Dear Vedran Smailovich, you are

my trial, my awful and untold truth and reconciliation, my hate/
    regret, my light of lights, the eternal kyrie eleison of our
        certain saintedness. And shame. And deity. Our meeting is
           the Serengeti of the soul. If her newborn
              wildebeest cannot stand alone, mother
           will leave her child behind. The Great Migration
              waits for no one. We are who
                we were. We are who
                  we are. Amen
                  and alas.

Studying a Film on the Treatment of Burns

The Black foreman tripped. One leg fell
 into the vat of boiling aluminum.
We take careful notes. We learn the treatment
protocols. We remove our glasses.
We are grateful for our hearing aids
which we will choose to do without. But
memories are burned into our eyes
and ears: The helpless lassoed with flaming
tire necklaces of gasoline
in Africa. Pan Am passengers
drifting in pieces from the English skies.
It is a lovely summer day.

Forward three months. The foreman's leg has healed.
Brown boiled melanin has been remastered into
tea-rose pink. Other than that, it's said to be all right.
The foreman thanks the doctors. He feels lucky.
He goes on. He returns to work.
Others die in other fires. Ghost-
witnesses, waiting patiently
to speak. They come to us at night.

Annual Pigeon Shoot, Higgens, PA.

This morning, Labor Day, the news
at seven finds me half-listening,
waiting for the promised
habañera of Bizet, and later
for a new orchestral Gaité
Parisienne. A bomb has caused
'collateral damage' somewhere
in the Middle East (that means
that children have been killed).
Florida warns its residents:
the con men are slithering
in the wake of the looters
across the path of rubble
of the first Fall hurricane. *Of course.
What else? Soon Bizet. Then Offenbach.*
But one more item before
the weather for Boston and vicinity
*(will it warm up enough
to have the usual barbecue?)*
From Higgens, Pennsylvania, we learn,
the annual pigeon shoot is underway.
*(People shooting pigeons? Well, perhaps
they are a plague, a Tiananmen Square
of raucous birds, carriers of disease...)*
The newscaster continues: The way
it's done, he says, is fixed by ritual.
Crammed into crates, the birds
are starved. Thus, a very few
can fly when freed. Those get away.
The others are shot dead. Presumably,
it doesn't take too long. Plenty
of time to picnic. Probably
the winner gets a prize. This year
there are a few protesters,

bussed in from New York.
The mayor is annoyed. New York, of all
places! People should learn
to tend to their own back yards!
Mind their own business, and leave
each to his own.

Inside Looking Out

Through the slatted shutter, or
the fluttering of a pale peach curtain, I
glimpse a small white dog (poodle? terrier?) leaping,
light with freedom. The owner stands by, benignly.
Lovely day. Summer sun reflected in
puddles of last night's shower. Laughing girls
as background music. Truck horns on an unseen
highway. Doppler of a distant freight
train. Mozart from an open window.

Who would have thought it! Sudden as
a nightmare, springing from the nowhere
of *once* and *when*, black mouth gaping, a wild
mangy creature (wolf? coyote?) wraps teeth
around dog collar as you or I might deftly
loop crochet hook into wool. Blood, cotton balls
of fur, guts, bones in slivers, shrieks and barks,
howls and the soft sound of children weeping. Is
this *my* dog? *Was* this my dog?

Nightmare

"What you fear most has already happened"
Annie G. Rogers

Like it or not
you come to me.

Lightning strikes
the lone tree and
the nomad under
it. I am incinerated
because s/he sought
shelter before the Rules
were laid down. *Learn
from experience,* hisses
Mother Wind. But it
is too late. *Be forewarned,*
moans Father Thunder,
after the fact.

Like it or not
you come to me,
night mentor.

Merciless oracle,
apostle of Truth,
you prophesy the past.

Letter to King Tut

We of this era, we ordinary people, stop by your sarcophagus, heart-struck. Dead in your teens, you are a boy like ours, still in highschool, trying out for soccer. Married at nine, a boy like ours, practicing the trumpet. Father of two stillborn daughters, a boy like ours, teasing his sister. We hope you knew your body would be held forever, preserved, protected – layer upon layer of nested gold to swaddle you as once your mother did, surrounded by your choice of jewels and your most favorite things. Our sons would choose their I-pods. Cell-phones. Laptops. Their favorite DVDs. A large supply of batteries.

We of this era, we ordinary people, live to raise our children, and to watch them get tipsy on their first baby's smile, to chase their toddlers, to read them "Goodnight Moon" just once more. As we did, long ago. Now we read with glasses honed exquisitely to fit our fashionable frames. We choose among the many types of contact lenses. We send our corneas to be lasered into shape, our cataracts to be zapped into oblivion. Our teeth, filled with gold, silver and the thinnest of ceramic, mate with transplants of anonymous bone from banks of dead bodies. We are partly made of metal: knees, hips, heads and spines, more every year. We owe our heartvalves to butchered pigs. We hear each other's softly whispered lovewords courtesy of twin computers hidden in our aging ear canals. Perhaps my chest will open to a heart newly harvested like an exotic fruit from a young man like you, victim of some grisly accident or crime, living on as if that heart were mine. But finally, I will die. And my husband. And our children, and their children.

Of something. Of life itself.

continued

If you are what you believe
        your *ba-soul* and *ka-self* live on
                one with your *akh-*
                      eternal-spirit sparkling
                              in the starry realm
                                      of the certainty
                                              of your great *Ra-Sun*

        enduring   unchanging   eternal

If we are what we cannot believe,
  Our restive *akhs* mutate
        from cloud to cloud, curious
                shape to curious shape
                        our homeless *ba's* and *ka's*
                              fading out, lonely
                                      as question marks

        generation   to   generation.

Who will study us as we study you?

Strange Meeting II

"I am the enemy you killed, my friend."
—Wilfred Owen

Words
ping off my shoulders
insist
around my head
set off short-circuits, storming every orifice.
Neurons fire, landmines in the blood.
This is a war, and I am afraid
You, true friend, become my enemy.

you   **to**
  everything   **know**
distinguish   perceive   discern
       me   **want**   **I**
to have sexual intercourse with
(see the Bible)
your   **recover**   **about**   **mem-**
re-
recouperare
ories
cover
revive
The task is
(to rise from the dead)
to bring to mind

Silence.
Bombs sprout parachutes
drift
graceful as leaves
In the morning mist we still do not forget
the anthem of the Kristallnacht.
This is a war, and I am safe.
You, old enemy, become my friend.

September 11, 2001

HERE ON EARTH
(before)

Here on earth

we need air
water
fire, and
spirit. *Here*

on earth we
need air. The oak
trees crack open
yellowbeige bare
broken in angles
of hurricane. *We*

need water. Floodings
of mud in basements,
carrying off our computers
our photographs our dishes
our life savings. *Here*
on earth we need

fire. Volcanoes sweeping
towns into dustbins, pets
and livestock and the
occasional human being
who couldn't get out in
time. *Here on earth*

we need spirit.
Here on earth.

HERE ON EARTH
(after)

Here on earth

we need air
water
fire, and
spirit. *Here*

on earth we
need air. Peace
shatters in rainbow
storms of bloody
glass bullets
and severed hands. *We*

need water. Punctured
sewer pipes, mouths
and ears and noses filled
with fetid excrement
of man and rat. *Here*
on earth we need

fire. We/they smash
buildings/bodies into
tombstones, ashes of
asbestos and the bones
and bones and bones of our
children. *Here on earth*

we need spirit.
Here on earth.

Kaddish for September

The sun deceives you, rising
as it does, predictably, at 6:20,
September 11, 2002. Like-
wise, the end of summer hijacks
you again with memories
of your childhood, of playing
outside after school, not much
in the way of homework. No
tests to study for. The scent
of Concord grapes.
                     Wednesday
this year. Day 254. The page
turns, its orderly processional
marching forward. Labor Day.
The Autumn equinox. And it's
someone's birthday, one
year older, of course.

      Rosh Hashana.
      Yom Kippur.
      Sukkoth.
      The school year.

      Where am I?
      Where are you?

Quivering in the vanilla teardrop
of the Yahrzeit candle, in
the spirit of that beautiful Tuesday
morning when sunshine and sky fused
into scimitars of shockwaves
pinning us to the ground zero
of our particular map. *Right
here* is where I was. On my tread-

mill, watching the morning news.
In my office answering e-mail. At
my kitchen table: Paying bills.
Drinking coffee. Listening to Bach

    When I heard.
    When I saw.
    When I knew.
    When I knew I knew.

          The murdered day
grows no older. The dead stay dead.
Unburied, they are echoes of smoke,
trace elements of DNA, a melted
wedding ring, a gold tooth. Sunset
is at 7:01. We go on, only
because we do. We fill
the distance that will widen,
like it or not.   Already
the forgetting has begun.
Boys with unchanged voices
are shouting in the playground.
Inevitably they will turn 18
and leave home. Inevitably
the last survivor of the Holocaust
will die off.

    Antietam, September 17,
    1862. New York/Washington/
    Pennsylvania. September 11,
    2001.

"If you can't say something nice, don't say anything at all"

— mother's advice

darkness drifts

    down   slow

        impartial snow

covering the graves of murderer and murdered. One and

the same. Liestruth. Daffodilsdandelionscrocuses blasting

green and yellow out of cracks of dead winter mud brown.

Do you love me? O yesno!

Mayday*

They're falling
falling clusters
clusterbombs   feathers
feathers   blood   ducks dropping
dropping dead   shot
shot mid-air
mid-air blood showers
showers   hail
hailstones   blood
blood-streaked stones felled to earth
earthquake flood fire
fire pyre crematorium
crematorium   where you
you mother father
fathermother of you
you friend wife husband   dead
dead on these pages
pages of children pages
pages pictures poems
poems   pages   remembrances
remembrances of the fallen
fallen, all fallen
fallen all.

---

* The etymology of Mayday is from the French, "M'AIDER" or M'AIDEZ", namely, "help me".

Moose Run River, New York City

Still
the moose chomps, unafraid,
in Macys, mindless of the mothers/pick-
pockets crushed into pie-wedges
of the revolving doors. She
stands, certain in the stony water,
harrumphing noisily. It is August.
She has forgotten about the lottery:
Come September, seven days are open
season. She will be shot standing there,
waiting for a cab that will agree

to take her to the Bronx. It's me
O Lord, canoeing along 23rd
street with my violin. On the IRT
I paddle downstream to 14th to bag
a seat on the express train up-
town. It's me, O Lord, rolling my wet
jeans, laughing at the loons
playing tag on the cross-town Pelham
Parkway bus. Left hand on strap,
I memorize atomic tables. Life

or death? A or B, O Lord? A deer
quivers into the brush. A rabbit dives
for cover under the dock. The moose
stands. She has not noticed yet
the lookout posted in the stairwell. She
has not seen the rapist in the hall,
or the mother smashing her baby daughter's
head against the wall. Any day
now, Fall begins. Meanwhile, summer
shimmers on the river. Hatpins

make the subway safe. Chlorine lets
us swim. Polio and AIDS are old
news. Bergen-Belsen was in Viet-
nam. Longer skirts are in. *Driving
home, the guide steers his truck care-
fully around a wiggling pink dot. It is
a butterfly, he says, stuck in its lunch-
time raspberry feast. Most folks round here,
he says, come for the fishing. But, he adds,
almost all of them throw the fish
back.*

Psalm 10B

Why, O Lord, do you stand far off? Why do you hide yourself in time of trouble?

Find me a place
to seek
the questions
to ask.

Find me a quiet place.
The questions will
resonate like
kyries in
the air of St. Marks
cathedral.

Find me names
to call on
when You still
have no answers
to the old
entreaties.

Find me names
to call on
when Your voice
echoes incoherently
in an alien
tongue.

Progress

The hill is always steep.
Sometimes it's icy, or deep-
scarred with trenches of last winter's

freeze-defrost cycle.
Or it's slicked grey with rain.
Or blistered with dried mud.

Whatever. Even in
the best of times it's always been
too much for my old car, or

now, this morning, for
my two-year old Toyota. Too
new, I think, to lose the war

again. My right
ankle aches, driving all night
pressing, always pressing against

the pedal, winning one
more inch, or not. It's (almost)
the same dream, (almost) the same

dreamer, (almost) the same
sleep.

Elegy

At the moment
of my death
the earth stops,
a dirigible
suspended over
the highway.

Such a clear day!

Notice how
I disappear.
Without me,
sweet singers, you
cannot rest, rocking
in the gentle arms
of the final triad.

The oboe sounds its A.

No longer major,
no longer minor,
the overtones come
alive with echoes.
The hollow fifth
is now the home

of my last breath.

Memorial Service for a Quaker

In the end she wanted you to know
what mattered. So she spoke inhabiting
the tender shallow spaces between the keys
of the clavier, between
the shards of grass, the in-
and-out-breaths in this Meeting
House. Here we wait,
patient iambs, graceful anapests
of faith, of awe, and witness, and of doubt,
the steady heartbeats of a sonnet thrumming
to the easy laplap of a summer
lake.

In the end she wanted you to know
it had been hard: Holding truth still
against the executioners, when
their blades were rusty with old blood. Coming
back. And back. And back. And back to tortures
untallied, terrors indescribable,
unforgettable. Therefore
forgotten. After, she insisted upon
apple trees. She mined for love, exalted
in the precious metals of her friends,
her family, the stunning souls of strangers.
She panned for joy. You were surprised to find
her in the cracks of driveways, springing up
yellow in fortunes of stubborn dandelions.
In summer she swayed purple in panoramas
of loosestrife, vibrated in fanfares
of red wild roses. You saw her soaring
with startled seagulls and the common Canada
goose. In the end, she wanted you
to know she was afraid to die alone
in the aftermath of ancient arrows,
knives, and hatchets. Forever, it seemed,
the butcher waited with the violent, vicious
ax.

In the end she wanted you to know
what matters now: glimpses of baby moose,
prancing silver in your headlights.
A grandchild with your toes.
An arm flung on your belly
in mid-night. Stars
that shock your skin, like lemon
ice exploding on your tongue. A prayer
hurled into silence. A kiss that loves you into
morning. A certain song: *Sometimes I feel
like a motherless child. Some-
times.*

Part 3

and

Mobile

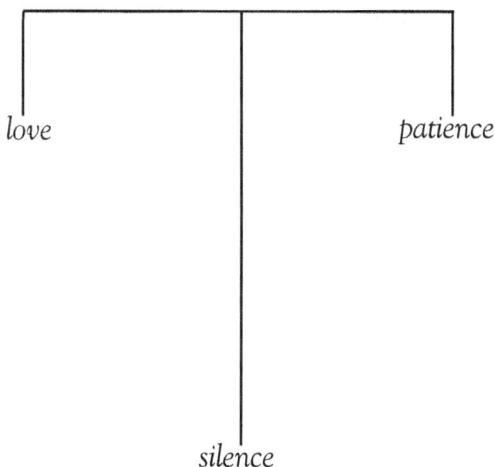

Cycle: Alfred, Maine

This year I wear red Gore-Tex, LL
Bean, via UPS. You
wear Winter, star-shower white
from the time before time
counted. The pond is icing
over, silver roofing on
another world. The moose are rutting.
The moles are burrowing. The squirrels
are scurrying. Santa has stopped
shaving. The partridge is caroling in
the pear tree. The robins are long gone.
Mosquitoes are a memory

to be recovered, come July. I hang
my jacket in the closet, where it will not
migrate, burrow, screw, scurry,
shave, sing, or bite. One day its
industrial zipper will stick for the last
time. Farewell. Hello, replacement,
whatever you are made of. The moose
have mated. The moles are burrowing.
The squirrels are scurrying. Santa has
stopped shaving. The partridge is caroling
in the pear tree. The robins are
long gone. Mosquitoes are a
memory.

Quaker Meeting: Cambridge/Rangeley, Maine

There you are, purchasing
  the Sunday paper. Ibuprofin.
    Ajax. Pampers. Peanut butter.
      Margerine. Clorox. There
you are, baby squalling, holy
  voices in the IGA,
    in Sarah's kitchen tasting oatmeal-
      raisin bread, yearning
for pies and chocoate frosting. You
  will not forget the Wednesday corn
    line. You must choose: How
      many? and are the kernels
small and sweet?

              'Almost died,' he
said, 'fever of 106, down to
the hospital.' 'Going to rain, trees
need the water, I guess.' 'Thanks be
to God, my son got out, the night my store
burned down.' 'Geologist dug up this
here rock, said it was from the time
of the Grand Canyon. Used to be this land
was all under water, back then.'
'Learned me the Internet at
the library - looked up my condition
on the Medline, they call it. Ain't
no reason, just old age, they say, doctors
don't know, but I'd have gone blind, it said,
if they hadn't of given me the Cortisone
in time.' 'I'll think on it awhile, let
you know if I can fix it for you.' 'The locksmith
out Rt. 4, he was a Baptist preacher,
died last June, you know. The schoolbus driver
he's out 16 across from where the diner was,

the widow sold him all the molds. Lock
stock and barrel, you could say.' 'Those wasps
you got, just spray 'em with Raid and run
like hell.'

Assessment Instrument

In the id there is nothing corresponding to the idea of time, no recognition of the passage of time.... Sigmund Freud, *New Introductory Lectures In Psychoanalysis*, 1933

>This is (only) a test. Take out your pen and paper.
>Without thinking (is that possible?)
>write as many words as (you can bear to) come to mind
>for each of the below:
>
>   (1) love *(5-second pause)*
>   (2) peace *(5-second pause)*
>   (3) truth *(5-second pause)*
>
>Your name is optional.
>There is no score-sheet.
>There is no score.

---

* *The Standard Edition of the Complete Psychological Works of Sigmund Freud*, V. 14, On the History of the Psycho-Analytic Movement, Papers on Metapsychology and Other Works, p. 296

From Afar (In Maine)

From afar our cabin door doesn't
creak. That restaurant that closed last year
could still be in business. The country market
may or may not sell fresh corn. There
are no mosquitoes or black flies. Though,
if you squint, you can make out a logging truck
amidst a string of match-box cars, and
a miniature moose galloping between
the swaying shoulders of Route 4. Parallel
lines almost converge. Faces have
been disappeared by distance. Therefore, none

of the invisible has died. Nor
has been born. Neither love nor hate
disturbs the shore-built homes, infests the fixer-
uppers on the hill, the A-frames by
the ponds, the hidden hunting lodges. How
the library continues to command
its sidestreet! But on their porches and their motor
boats, who is reading what? The air
is full of secrets. Who is crying? Are
the loons calling?

I remember driving down the Cross-
Bronx Expressway, cannibalized Nash's
rusting out, broken bottles cradled
by pock-marked hubcaps on the off-ramp
just after I left home, married at 20.
1959. From afar
the Projects, and their modern condo cousins
stand ramrod equal. Today, in
the democracy of distance wait a thousand
eyes unblinking, blinds arranged just so.
I imagine another me, throwing

lifeline after lifeline to the self
imagining. *She* (reading, sleeping,
cleaning, watching tv) does not see
me, hear me calling her. Old/young
woman, still in her stand-up kitchen,
we pass, anonymous. *Come to me!*
the loon sings out. *Come to me*, mail
carrier, toll collector, maid, bus
driver, woodcutter, baker, sweeper of
the city streets. Without you this
is no poem at all.

Naming

Apple! He tastes the syllables
again, hearing *red, green,*
smelling *sweet with sweet white juice.*
Wordless, his one-year-old fingers
punctuate the air, towards
the refrigerator. *Hah!*
(*There! In there!*)

Wanderers in the Museum of
Antiquities we find ourselves attended
by the ancient Buddhas of Tibet,
by way of China. Gazing down they watch
kindly over us, the unenlightened.
We are tutored by the bodhisattvas,
humble heroes whose names we can't pronounce.
Gladly they waited here on earth, postponing
Nirvana for the sake of those who needed
them. For us. Patience beyond patience.
Blessing beyond blessing. Names beyond names.

In the beginning was the Word

        And the Word,

infinite   unspoken   unspeakable
    rises,
        rises,
              a transparent
helium
        balloon
              a
                    coda of
    ethereal
        echoes

just   out of reach

                              disappearing

              like fog   at sunrise.

                          Truth?
or mirage?

                       Who are you

God, Jehovah, Supreme Being, Almighty, Everlasting, Eternal, King
of Kings, Creator, Yahveh, Adonai, Allah, Buddha, the Atman,
Brahma, Goddess. The Spirit. The Light. The Nameless One.

                    I am that I am,

          wearing a necklace of old Greek
          coins, silver full moons
          against a dark blouse sky. My newest
          grandson, five months into life,
          leans into his future, fingers
          already expert at the grab. *Ah
          GAH!* he shouts. *(I want it!)*

Deconstruction: 'I Know Why The Caged Bird Sings"
(Maya Angelou)

I
Center of my maypole, I
am the descendent of Eve
and Hildegard, and of Odetta.
I am she of the lullabye
and the nigun, of aria
and ballad, of spiritual, of Bread
and Roses, and the honest Shaker
hymn. You may have heard me
chanting in the back seat
of taxis, and the bow of birch
canoes, caroling in kitchens
and in launderettes, whistling
Chopin by the side of
the chlorinated swimming pool
(dreaming of dolphins), humming on
backyard tire swings and
subway platforms.
You hear me celebrating births
and birthdays in languages
I do not speak. You will always
hear my dirge as the body
is lowered in the broken ground.

know
How do I know? in the sweep
of sound I am yours. You reach
satori and I shimmer with you.

why
Because I must. Because you must.

the
The bird. A bird. Still *the* bird.

caged
Behind bars, she has chosen
life. Life is freedom. *Free
   as a bird.* Freedom
is life. We cannot always
unlock the cage. Is there air?

bird
sparrow, pigeon, egret, owl,
heron, hawk, blue jay, chicken,
parrot, nuthatch, robin, goose.
Birds fly. Feathers and wings.
   White dove: bird of peace.

sings
One magical March day, I,
beige lady, on vacation,
possessed by possibility,
improv with a band of Black
men in a park in New
Orleans. Clarinet, slide
trombone, sax, guitar, steel
drum. Each in turn is master
of his 3-line message. We
others wait, respect married
to ecstasy. Now I feel
the heat of an arm around me, bass
player pinging with his other
index finger. The clarinet
and horn caress that sweet diminished
fifth, holding the whole world's
breath. The universe is mine.
I float my soprano riff.

Kingdom is Come. For a moment
we all dissolve, skin-
hair-eyes-bones man/
woman, young/old/, brown/
black/beige/ tourist/all-
their-life-playing-blues-guys
and the music wraps us up
    tight as a rocket.

In honor of the musicians of New Orleans

Calling

my dream dreams on in its dreamlogic   cows
are turning into people *cower*   *coward*   people
long dead are young again in countries their hungry
eyes have never seen   no man (woman) is *an island*
an is-land *an eye-land*   *an I-land*   I wander   the
landscape   sadness dusts the leaves my old friend Ferdinand ambles by
smelling the flowers   a *llama* led by a brain-
damaged girl lopes by my house   I am reminded
of a Lama's practice of Tonglen   *breathe in the pain*
of the world   *your pain is my pain*   *breathe out*
compassion   *for you*   *for me*   *for you*
         for me

I hear you calling me   far away but clear   clear
zen gongs   the dingdong of your iv apparatus   my
name   *marian, marian*   *in your sleep, in*
my sleep.

Bed

        is our parenthesis of
        life lived by daylight
        in cars, at kitchen tables,
        at desks, in chairs and sub-
        ways, in bathtubs, on stepladders
        and toilets. On good August days

there are kayaks and canoes down wild Maine rivers. There are star-shot lakes ringed by piney fragrances fused with unborn wines of blueblack raspstraw-berries. On good April days there are jets to Spain, lunch in first-class compartments on the fast train to Barcelona, red rioja with every course. On good days there are Venezuelan beaches, Rockettes of flamingos courting us, the February salt air humming in our nostrils. Always, wherever, kind bed, you hold us tight in the clasp of sheets and comforters. We

        dream, curved in your night
        arms. We wake to your cozy
        crinkle, your welcoming groan,
        your greeting to first light, your
        reminder that today we have one
        more one last chance.

Advice

*Do not ask yourself, "**What** do I see?" Rather, ask, "What do **I** see?"**

        cruelty in
        a barn
        door. Love
        in a silent
        oboe. Grief
        in the ripest of
        strawberries.
        Loyalty and
        honor in a vase
        of wilting daisies.
        Joy in an old torn
        stocking. Doubt
        and faith in a ravel-
        ing sweater. Trust
        in the invisible
        light, yours
        and not-yours.

*Richard Schmid, *Alla Prima: Everything I Know About Painting*

Little Ghost

Do you ever notice as you write that no matter what there is on the written page something appears to be in **back of everything that is said, a little ghost**....*It has the shape of your own soul as you write.* *

    Here I am!
         inside the curl of your hair
         between your breasts
         in the space between two of
         your neighbor toes,
         the pause between in-breaths
         and out-breaths, pulse
         beats, eye-blinks, wrinkles,
         the recesses of your belly-
         button. Imagine a symphony
         of rests! Imagine painting
         with bristles of air! Hello,

    dear ghost!
         Sing me a song of spaces,
         spin me a sweater of button
         holes, a carpet of woven
         woolen pores, serve me
         sieves of sugar, funnels of wine.

---

* Barbara Guest, *American Poetry Review*, Sept./Oct 2002, 31:5, p. 13

ER, IV, EKG, CAT, BP...

Letters float, genderless
angels, wings sheer as dragonflies
whose airy bodies circled our canoe
last August on the Concord River.
Almost out of human range, their tiny
cymbal voices sang to us, hmm-ing
round and round, soprano guardians
asking nothing of us at all.

Dragonfly, I hear you
in the hum of the heart monitor, in
the sigh of the blood pressure bulb
as it exhales, in the spongy soles
of the nurse's shoes, the squeal
and squeak of the dinner cart. *Unto
us you are given*. For no reason,
free, and without indemnity.

Time Travel

Before you died
we'd found an hour
to meet, so-called
free time between
the lines. Work
commitments; the
inevitable dentist,
rheumatologist,
cardiologist,
opthalmologist,
podiatrist,
physical therapist.
The plumber. Finally,
Friday at 2:00.

This time it was
the hospital.
A problem. Some
damned tests or other.
We rescheduled,
sighing, as usual.
Wednesday at noon,
two weeks hence.
Time to talk. About
anything. Every-
thing. I'll bring
the coffee, yours
black.

How shall I tell you?
Sandwich in hand, you
don't seem to know
you died last month.

Wednesday at noon.
Here we are,
you in your Harvard
rocking chair,
I in the chipped
yellow Eames,
grandfather of the molded
models linked like paper
doll cut-outs, bolted
to the floors of airports
everywhere. How
can I tell you? Would
you want to know?
Does it
matter?

Birthday

On his next birthday, my dead friend
appears in my dream. All of us –
my husband, his wife, and I –
are celebrating at the best
French restaurant in town. Alive,
we order carefully, counting
calories, avoiding salt,
saturated fat, meat,
and certain spices. No wine,
lest it confound our opiates,
our sleeping pills, and antihistamines.

Now 84, my friend is laughing,
ordering creamed soup, shrimp,
and the rarest steak with bearnaise,
champagne followed by merlot,
and frosted chocolate cake, vanilla
ice cream and hot fudge sauce.
Espresso, despite the lateness of the hour.

Healed at last. Diabetes,
heart disease, deceased. Low-fat
diets buried. By-passes,
pace-maker, defibrillator,
cardiac ablations, toes
amputated, unwanted naps in
the afternoon: Over. Canes.
Walkers. Rehabs. Instead
of tennis shoes and long hikes
with the dog.   On summer days

heat arrows from the sidewalk in serrated stainless swords.
Evenings offer us its slender teardrops of liquid silver rain.

Visitation

I almost saw You
that is, I saw Almost-You
hurrying through the automatic doors
of the stop&shop, disappearing
into the hornets nest of carts/strollers/
walkers/mini-baskets, armed only with
a plastic bag. Later I saw Almost-
You again at the healthclub,
doggedly doing laps. Crawl up,
backstroke down. Crawl up, backstroke
down. Almost-You glanced my way
as I side-stroked by, three lanes over
both of us ageless
in the weightlessness of water.

The thing is,
I cannot bring myself to wave
and say hello, or hold the door, or wish
Almost-You a good day, or a happy
new year. Almost-You would say
'thank you' or 'the same to you.' But
Almost-You answering Someone-Me
doesn't know Me. Doesn't miss
Me. Doesn't know You. Couldn't
care less. *Have a good day,*
I say at last. *You too,* says Almost-
You, heading for the showers. But
what *good day* is it?
And what country? In what year?

April in Paris: Sur Le Metro

I'm on the train with you again. But now a slim
young man has taken your place in front of me,
swaying gracefully, one hand on pole, i-pod in
pocket, ear-bud in ear. The accordian-player croons
songs in languages I don't know well enough to
translate, juggling his paper coffee cup of euros,
sashaying deftly to the next car, without falling.
Amore. Amour. Amor. These words I know.

Where did you go? When did you get off? Surely
you didn't mean to leave me on the jump seat *réservé*
for *les handicapés!* I make my way, pocketbook and
plastic bag in hand — Evian, apple, pocket *dictionnaire* —
to the *possibilité* of *renversement*. Where am I now?
Je ne sais pas. And you? Perhaps *en route* to
our *petit pension*. *S'il vous plaît, Madame, où est
la direction Balard, à fin de la ligne violet?*

In the *correspondance* I recognize the homeless
woman curled around her blanket, her head
bolstered by floral rags. The fruit and flower stand is
busy with bananas, dates, and strawberries. Lilies
flirt with tulips, their stems drinking together in
tall tin water cans. Bits of trash, like sparrows,
congregate near overflowing bins. People hurry,
vite, vite, a flash of *rouge* toenails, scalpel-sharp

high heels in step with *traductions* of beige
Birkenstocks. And there's the harp we heard
this very morning, accompanied by amplified CD,
sailing Bach's Praeludium on the absent ocean.
Overhead, each note a silvery balloon, Gounod's
Ave Maria floats through my memory's life sky,
always the perfect lover, the perfect marriage,
the *anniversaire* of the uncounted and uncountable.

Wake me up now! Let me find you at the next
platform. Let me find you studying your subway
map, planning another afternoon at some *musée*
we haven't seen. Let me find you, just across
the track, waiting for me.

La Touriste San Souci

Nightmares do not follow me today.

My pocketbook has not been stolen, nor
is it lost. Somehow it's safely stowed,
and I can stride or even skip, my way
down *la petite Rue D'Amelie*, swinging
my arms. O dear freedom! O *chère liberté!*
Elevators stay their course, clean
bathrooms appear as needed, and *beaucoup
gendarmes* smile at me and tip their caps.
I've lost my *carte* and phrasebook, *c'est vrai*,
but strangers speak English, falling into step,
taking my arm, pointing out their favorite
sights. My highschool French buys me *une pomme*
with some loose coins that show up in my pocket.
De l'eau? I am directed to a nearby
water cooler.

Now it's time to meet my lover *à
l'Hôtel Les Jardins d'Eiffel*. He
has not forgotten. He has not died.
He is waiting for me, out front
on the hotel steps, waving, waving
and holding out his arms. I don't need flowers.
I don't need chocolate, I don't need coffee,
or even sunlight in my world. *Je n'ai pas
besoin des fleurs. Je n'ai pas besoin
du chocolate. Je n'ai pas besoin
le café, ou même la lumière
du soleil dans mon monde.*

Ice Season on the Reservoir

Ice creeps in
dream of kittens
little white feet
quiet, so quiet you'd
hardly notice them.
Autumn slips
over us while we're
sleeping. Lapis water
fades to dirty laundry
grey to black and blue.
A bruise, glowing
with pain.

Like the pupil
of an eye, however,
the center holds. A duck
or two stay, waiting,
waiting. Flapflap
flapping their wings they tend
their tiny pond. Flap
faster! I pray, silently.
Fly south, or flap
faster.

Last Assignment (*with guitar*)

Rumor has it
that the *devas* have deserted us.
We alone remain, outliers
in the boondocks of old age,
solving riddles without the help
of those who came before us. Frailing
for the first time, your fingers
bleed. Your nails crack and splinter.
Even when they're looking right
at you, your children cannot know
the cost of what you're doing, why
you're doing it, or that they too
will have to do it by themselves
when their turn comes.

(Note: *'frailing'* is a technique used by guitar and banjo players)

Keepsake

The reckless wind has captured one old
faux-gold earring, kiting it
from my left ear, out the driver's window
of my new car, parachuting
to the street. A tiny *clink*. Shall
I stop to rescue this chipped
metal bird? Once she may have sung
a lovesong that I danced to. Take
her in. Mend her wing. Put her back
in her box, with her mate.

Packing

After a long stay, they
are packing up. It's
been a lifetime since
they came. At first
they didn't have much
furniture, none
at all, in fact. But
now there are beds,
tables, bureaus, desks,
dishes, everything
they needed, and more than
they needed, more every
year. It's hard work
packing crates, bales,
and boxes, but it can
be done. Everyone
has to do it sometime,
and everyone succeeds

in the long run. You
thistle, you amber
day lilies, Queen Anne's
lace, golden rod,
you dandelions sprouting
in the concrete sidewalk
cracks, you will not
survive the trip. Farewell,
misted springtime walks,
vanilla-scented clover
underfoot. Farewell, Sweet
William, fragrant apple
blossom, dearest phlox....
They'll take the glass
vase, however. Care-
fully they wrap it in old
newspaper. Is the vase
empty? Is it not?

Choosing a Seat

suppose i always sit in the same place more or less then you
can find me without opening your eyes without being there at
all i am where i should be every sunday morning at the meeting
house on the center bench across from you and every second
wednesday of the month in the committee room in the straight-
backed chair and next to you at the quaker writers group and in
my office just opposite from you and eating breakfast together
at the kitchen table and in the invisible air between our cell phones
and just behind you choosing apples at the farmers market and at
my desk paying bills....and even if i am not there i am there in your
mind and therefore i am there because you are there in my mind.

> *Look for me!* I will not forget
> to come. Every time, without
> fail, I will be there with you.

Pure Love

To my grandfather, Edward (Isaak) Kaplun,
b. 18 April, 1880. d. 31 May, 1955

your love flies
across the centuries
on the backs of camels
and whales your
letters   dance, spin strong with   the
swirls   of your oldfashioned handwriting   elegant
windswept sssssssssss's, caterpillars of
mmmmmmmmm's and nnnnnnnnnnnnn's, gaggles of gggggggs
and pppppppppppp's, stanchions of lllllllllllllllllllllll's,
portholes of ooooooooooo's
constellations of   stellar
specks   ballooning   skyward
set free from   i's and   j's
on the other side of the invisible world
where we are both perfect,
where you live

and where you love me from

!!AFTER?? ?

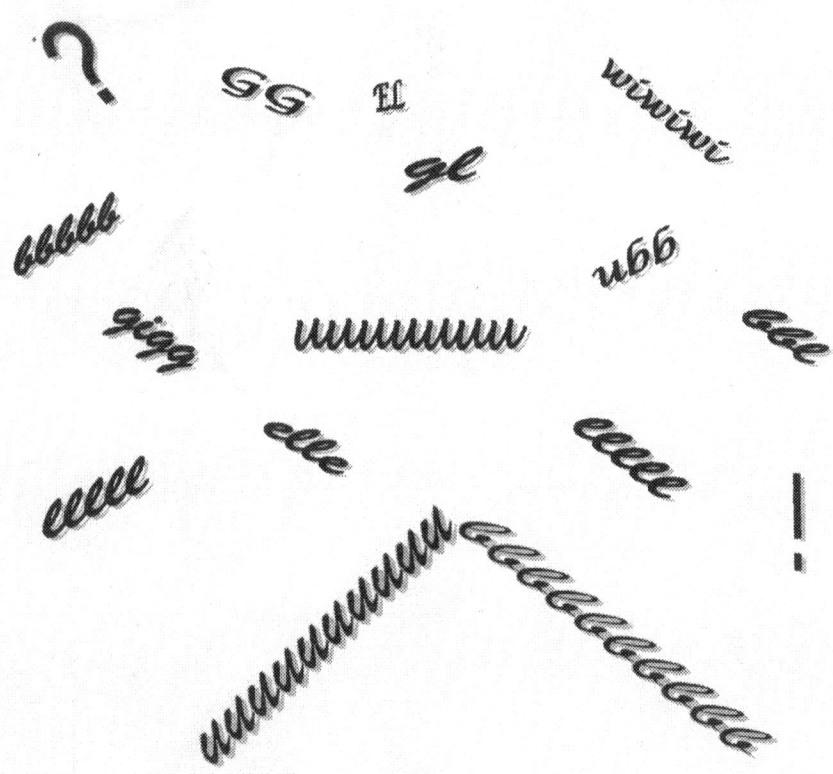

Inheritance

My grandfather, a violinist, said
"Play for the one who knows."

My father, his student, said, "Play
for the one who knows."

I, my father's student, say, "Play for
the one who knows." Who knows

who is the one who knows?

The Sculpture Garden

"I enjoy carving best of all the things I do. It's a good life changing dreams into stone."
    —John Tiktak, (1916-1981) Inuit artist
"In the very first times...both people and animals lived on the earth, but there was no difference between them...a person could become an animal, and an animal could become a human being."
    —Naalungiq, Inuit elder

Over there is the section I call *Chased*, subsets of which include *by an animal*, such as lions, dogs, tigers, and angry elephants; and subsets of which include *by a human I know*, both those living and those dead, mother, for example; the visiting rapist; the crazed mugger, desperate for a fix; *by a human of ill repute:* Hitler, Son of Sam, David Koresh; and *by mythical monsters*: devils, werewolves, and vampires in whose existence my consciousness
does not believe.

To the left, *No Help*: the telephone that does not work; the stolen wallet; the car that does not start, late at night and far from home; the ambulance that will not come; the broken key, my last chance to escape eternal captivity in the prison of the forgotten. And worst of all, although I am alive, my body has been prepared for burial. It has been laid out, sealed in an air-tight coffin, and now it's being lowered in the ground. I cannot scream, I cannot move.
No way out.

To the right, a smaller piece, which you have probably seen elsewhere: *Exam*: failed, unfinished, late for, blown off. In that far corner is *Baby*: something wrong with. To one side, *Disease*: Ebola, for example. No treatment. Death entombed in pain. And then, up on the dais is *Airplane*: explosion   crash; you are familiar with those? A larger area for so-called *Acts Of God*: Hurricane, Earthquake, Forest Fire, Avalanche, Tornado, Tsunami: everything destroyed.
Everything.

An enclave of its own, edged by electric fences, is set aside for
War: subsets of *bombs*: atomic, car, suicide; *landmines*: note the bloody
bandages, the amputees, the burned skin, the smell of death, difficult
to infuse into pores of marble, but absolutely necessary. Zones marked
off for *genocides* of various ilks. Subdivisions for beheadings, rapes,
simple and exotic tortures. And, marked with your name, there is
a plot reserved for you, for your uneasy ghosts, your personal
night stalkers.

*I'm looking for your soul, John Tiktak. I'm looking for you, playing
with the otters, the seals, the caribou, your soul brothers, your soul sisters.
I'm looking for you, soaring with the snowy owl, the bald eagle, the grey-blue
heron, across the frozen river, the Fall air crisp as a Granny Smith.
I'm looking for the breath you continue to exhale, your eternal clouds
of mist, your islands of life's insistence,
world without end.*

Enjambment

What
does it matter where
the line ends? where the
line ends? where the line
ends? where the line ends?
What matters is whether
it continues on or
not.

I've
lost my pocketbook again, and all its contents:
wallet, cellphone, pda. Pills, shopping lists,
two crumpled coupons – half off sweaters at
Lord & Taylor, today only; 10¢ off Listerine.
What matters is the driver's license. Relieved,
I remember that a temporary copy can be printed
out on line, for a small fee, payable by credit card.
What matters is that I can drive. Whether or not
I know where I'm going or why, that I can
drive.

Leaves

parachuting through the cross-

winds of autumn, dancing

on remembrances of hurricanes

and summer thunderstorms

and spring drenchings and late-

May hail, and last March's

final blizzard and on intimations of

this winter's January ice-rain/

snow-showers and puffy mattresses

of softest whitewhitewhite

without surcease. November. You

are leaving.   December.

You have left. Where have you gone,

my friend? Where have you

gone?

Ellipses

        you know how it is...
                because, after all...   considering...
well, of course...   ...in those days
  not that he meant anything by it...
          better to forgive and forget...
...of course, of course...   it's water under the bridge...
  ...it was a shame...   if only he...
        we don't like to say...
    ...not right, though   I didn't know...
...too late   too late...
        ...to do anything anyway.

Life

and but why if when or how not

not how if why but and or

if and or why but how

why if but how and

but and why if

and but why

and but

and

and

and

and

and

About the Author

Born in 1939 in The Bronx (New York City), Marian Kaplun Shapiro received her B.A. in English (writing) from Queens College, and her Masters and Doctorate from Harvard. She lives in Lexington, Massachusetts, where she practices as a psychologist and poet. In addition to her poetry, she is the author of a book, *Second Childhood* (Norton, 1989), a chapter in *What Is Psychotherapy?* (Jossey-Bass, 1990), and in *Play* (Wiley, 2002) as well as of many journal articles.

As a young person, Marian was encouraged to write and publish by established poets such as Stephen Stepanchev, Stanley Kunitz, Alan Tate, and Archibald MacLeish. However, it is only in the last six years that she began to submit her work, and achieve publication in over 75 journals and anthologies, winning many (non-lucrative) prizes en route. She is constantly amazed at her good fortune, which includes her husband, two children, their loving spouses, and four delightful grandchildren. A Quaker, her poetry often reflects the splitscreen truths of violence and peace, doubt and belief, despair and abiding hope.

www.ingramcontent.com/pod-product-compliance
Lightning Source LLC
Chambersburg PA
CBHW071020080526
44587CB00015B/2433